Finding the Best Person for the Job:

Interview Guidelines and Techniques

T0342704

Graham Clinch

ETT Imprint & Svengali Press

First published 2018 by Svengali Press
Reprint 2019 by ETT Imprint & Svengali Press

PO Box 1852

Strawberry Hills

NSW 2012

AUSTRALIA

trilby@svengalipress.com.au

www.svengalipress.com.au

ISBN 978-0-994615-59-6 (pbk)

ISBN 978-1-925706-94-9 (ebk)

WITH THANKS

MY son Rob has a talent for asking pointed questions in the nicest possible way. After some discussions about conducting job interviews, he said: "Dad, it would be really great if you could jot down a few notes about some of these things. Could you do that?" And that was the very beginning of this book. He also maintained my motivation by telling me how he uses the ideas and processes in selecting key members for his team—both professional and support staff. Without his request and appreciation, it would not exist.

As we know, there is more to publishing than a simple request and encouragement. It takes exceptional dedication to maintain the focus for endless proof readings to ensure accuracy and avoid errors. But taking the time to understand the content and the context is even more essential for a reviewer and literary guide to be effective. I was most fortunate to have the support of my sister Dorothy Outram, an experienced writer and editor to fill this role and she did so spontaneously, with great energy and to outstanding effect.

Dorothy and her husband, Bill, also contributed many more resources to make this a truly professional publication.

Finally, to all those who trusted, challenged and worked with me in conducting job interviews over the years, "Thank you".

Graham Clinch

CONTENTS

1   The Ideal Interview   1

2   What Are We Looking For?   3

3   Preparation and Analysis   17

4   Productive Interviewing   24

5   Panel Interviews   39

6   Common Listening Traps   43

7   Common Assumptions   46

8   Closing Reflections   48

9   The Last Word   51

PREFACE

WHAT is the best way of choosing the "right person for the job"?

This small book explains how to identify people who will add value to your enterprise while fitting comfortably within the culture of your workplace.

Step by step, you will learn how to gather enough meaningful information to protect you from later discovering your appointee is anything but the person you thought you met at interview.

The book does not describe what makes a "good employee". That all depends on the role, the context and the current circumstances. But it does offer advice to help you make the **evidence-based decisions** that lead to "best fit" appointments for you and your team.

1

THE IDEAL INTERVIEW

INTERVIEWS are the platform we use for understanding the quality of an applicant's work: their ability to solve problems; their capacity to persevere in the face of daunting odds; their attitude to other people at all levels; and their commitment to sound principles and standards.

These are serious matters which can be difficult for an applicant to discuss in detail with someone they've only just met. Yet it is important that the interviewer obtain as much relevant information as possible in the time available.

In all the interviews I have attended, the most productive have been associated with first establishing a tone of mutual respect from which trust can readily flow. Some applicants will engage in this process naturally; some will respond if we give the lead; and a few will resist our invitation.

Let us remember, however, that the tone and structure of the interview are set by our own actions. This is not the time to show off our knowledge, achievements or opinions. It is the time to conduct a **dialogue** with the applicant. It is the time to genuinely **listen**—with eyes as well as ears. We learn nothing new when **we** are doing all the talking.

2

WHAT ARE WE LOOKING FOR?

INTERVIEWS work best when the content and process are kept simple. The broad areas we need to cover can be limited to three:

- Competence
- Compatibility
- Integrity

Competence

Can the applicant demonstrate the level of knowledge and expertise to perform in the role to the standards we require?

This process includes confirming qualifications and accreditations, currency of practice, and experience. We need to be clear and explicit **in our own minds** about the standards we are expecting and why. As the discussion starts to flow, we discuss how applicants have dealt with relevant challenging situations in their work roles, and ask about their main achievements.

3

Usually we work from the simple to the complex. One question at a time works best in most situations: the applicant can focus and we are in a good position to develop a chain of enquiry, record responses and develop the comprehensive understanding we need.

The following sequence of questions is likely to confirm to the applicant that we are genuinely interested in them and wish to ensure that the information we are relying on is both relevant and correct.

> *If I may, let me just check some of the detail we have about you, OK? Your qualifications are ..... ?*
>
> *You have been working at ... for ... years?*
>
> *And your current role is ... Is that correct?*

While this approach helps put the applicant at ease, it also offers the opportunity for them to update information if necessary: for example, a change of role, additional qualifications, or even a change of employment. And when there have been recent changes, they are frequently significant.

Then we might proceed to a question such as:

> *Would you please explain for us the main <u>contribution</u> expected from you (or made by you) in your current role?*

Sometimes we need to point out that a "contribution" is an outcome, not a "to do" list. A similar question could be:

What difference does it make (to the team or to the outcomes) when you carry out your role well?

And to get a better understanding, add questions, one at a time, such as:

What proportion of your time, approximately, do you spend on that?

How does the benefit of that contribution rate in proportion to the amount of time and resources you require for it?

What changes, if any, have you made, or suggested, to improve the quality of your contribution or the efficiency of your role?

To get more insight into an applicant's level of accountability or authority, use questions such as:

Who is involved in the overall process?

Where do you fit in that process?

What decisions do you make without having to seek authority from any other source? Could you give us a couple of examples, please?

What decisions do you usually make after consultation with others, even when you could make the decision unilaterally?

Would you describe the overall process as teamwork or individual contribution? Could you elaborate, please?

What works better for you—individual focus or more emphasis on being a team? Why is that?

How is communication managed within the team or work group? Who is ultimately accountable for it?

To learn about significant achievements at work:

What are the typical day-to-day achievements that give you the greatest sense of job satisfaction? Why is that?

What are some of your recent achievements which you consider to be above the average, more than what happens on a "day-to-day" basis?

Why was it considered a great achievement?

Look for the following, but do not prompt: the outcome; a brilliant or inspired individual contribution; a favourable cost/benefit ratio etc.

What have you learned from your biggest mistake in your career / professional life?

This question assumes the person has made mistakes—like all the rest of us. Learning from mistakes is more likely to indicate maturity and ongoing self-development than assertions of never having failed. Even though we generally oppose prompting, when an applicant is hesitant to admit to any mistakes, we might observe:

> *Actually none of us (the interviewers) actually know of anyone who has never made a mistake; it's how we respond to them that seems to make the difference.*

And give them a second chance.

Compatibility

Can the applicant demonstrate the ability and attitude to relate to others in a way which is mutually supportive and respectful?

Compatibility comes in the form of empathy and in the willingness to listen and adapt when the goals of the work unit require it.

Evidence to listen for:

- Use of personal pronouns: Is there a balance in the use of "I" and "we"? Did "we" achieve, or was "I" the only sound performer with "them" being the problem?

- Response to conflict: How has the person attempted to restore professional and meaningful work relationships after some form of conflict or difference of opinion?

The matter of compatibility is also addressed in several of the discussions explored in the previous section. For example, we typically learn much about:

- Whether or not the person works happily and effectively in a team environment.
- The extent to which they consider it important to communicate—too much or too little!
- Whether or not they see their role or contribution to be superior to that of others.
- When they talk about achievements, is recognition given to anyone else?
- When they talk about problems or failures, is fault found only in others?
- The extent of their insight into, and empathy for others. Does the applicant start with a reasonable assumption that others are also trying their best to achieve worthwhile goals?
- Their attitude towards "authority".

When compatibility matters come up in the earlier section about work roles and accountabilities, it is usually better to pursue them on the spot. Continuing with the flow of conversation is more natural than sticking to a more logically structured list and waiting for "the right section" to pursue them.

The matter of compatibility can also be pursued with questions such as the following, **asked sequentially**:

Who challenges you and your ideas in your role at work?

How does that work for each of you? What significant differences of opinion have you had to resolve?

How did you do that?

Note whether the applicant takes all the credit or describes a mutual process.

Have you ever had such a difference of opinion with another person that you have never worked with her or him again? Could you please tell us how and why that happened? Ask further specific questions as necessary.

How many work associates have you retained as colleagues even years after your career paths separated? (Ask them to "tell the story": who, how, and why.)

Who are the key people you work with who are in a position of lesser authority or professional status? How do you work together? Please give us a couple of examples of how differences of opinion are handled between you and them.

Can you please describe the attitudes and typical behaviour of the person you would least like to work with ever again in your life?

In responding to this question almost everyone describes a person who is opposite to themselves. It is highly productive because the applicant is expressing observations about someone else, but the content can reveal much more about the individual.

The question sequence works in the following way, but note that the wording is key to getting the desired result:

> *Interviewer: Can you reflect for a moment and think of the person you would least like to work with ever again. Don't tell me their name; just think of that person.*
>
> *If the applicant says something like: That's not a problem; I can work with anyone...*
>
> *Respond with: I'm sure you can. But if you had to list people in order of preference, whom would you put last on the list.*
>
> *When the applicant indicates they have a person in mind, ask: Now, without mentioning the person's name, please describe for me their behaviour, what that person actually did, that made it so difficult to work with them.*

And then we listen patiently to the observations our applicant makes. We don't interrupt or add our own "pearls of wisdom".

So, for example, a person who has high integrity and always tries to produce first class work will describe the least preferred co-worker as someone who is lazy, dishonest, self-serving, or in similar terms.

I have asked this question in literally hundreds of job interviews and the applicants consistently describe a person opposite to themselves. This has been verified by examining other well-founded information about them. Similarly, when the question is asked in group training sessions, the participants have the same type of reaction.

However, it is essential that the question be asked precisely as already indicated above:

*Can you reflect for a moment and think of **the person you would least like to work with ever again?** Don't tell me their name; just think of that person.*

Examples of further questions to help understand the applicant's typical attitudes and reactions to others include:

What are your typical clients / patients / customers like? (Note whether the themes in the overall response are positive or negative.)

Could you please describe for us the clash or conflict with a client / patient / customer that concerned you the most?

What did you do on your own initiative to attempt to resolve it?

And what was the ultimate outcome?

These four questions are asked sequentially, not simultaneously

Integrity

Does the applicant demonstrate consistency in the application of core values, both personally and as a team member?

Is integrity evident both in day-to-day matters as well as those where their self-interest might be at risk?

Are "the facts" of a matter used to solve problems rather than relying on witch hunts that avoid personal responsibility?

Insight into a person's integrity is found within the discussions about their work achievements, how they have solved problems and how they typically deal with other people. It is also evident in the balance they achieve between compliance with rules and procedures and their commitment to achieving necessary outcomes. Insistence on complying with procedures is not an example of integrity when it conflicts with the very purpose of those procedures when they were written.

When discussing professional ethics, for example, and the applicant is recounting a situation which involved a conflict of interest, we can ask:

What principles or beliefs guided you when the situation was most complex, at its worst?

And that should be followed up with questions such as:

Where else have such principles guided your decisions and actions?

How have you reacted when you could see that adhering to your principles would not be to your personal advantage? For example?

Can you explain for us how those guiding principles developed in you?

How do the principles you apply at work differ to those in other parts of your life? (If they are true principles, there should be no difference.)

The best way to get useful information about these essential qualities is to get people talking about their work. And that is a variable process. Some can't be stopped once they get started and we need to steer and direct them without coming across as abrupt or dismissive.

And then there are those who find it hard to start. I know people who are highly accomplished in their careers and who speak eloquently about the virtues of their team-mates yet find it awkward to present their own outstanding qualities. They need more time and a variation in approach. We will deal with this again later, but we can usually help people open up by focusing on the work they've done and what they and their team have accomplished. Then we can gradually bring the discussion back to their individual contribution.

Once we have established an easy flowing discussion and good engagement, it is amazing what people will tell us about the times they took the easy way out or used others unfairly to their own advantage. They will—if we listen. Often, they see their behavior as clever or shrewd and take a certain pride in it. We need to find out more. The following are just a few examples of statements calling for further exploration:

> *They didn't ask, and I didn't have to tell them*
> ...

> *As the accountant I can guarantee my boss will get whatever set of numbers is required ...*

> *Under the rules at the time, the responsibility lay entirely with another department ...*

> *The conditions of my contract stated that I was* ***entitled*** *to ... so I abided by those conditions.*

(Often used to justify a refusal to work flexibly with others or similar.)

> *I had done all I could in setting up the process for them; there was no point in hanging around to do the work for them.*

(This statement came from a person who left after three months into a twelve-month project. Alternative versions of this response are commonplace. They should always be explored.)

Constant references to:

... a matter of principle ... or

... it was a health/safety/security issue ...

can be an indication of a person who abides by the letter of the law regardless of the core issues and genuine needs of the situation.

Frequent job changes can be a warning sign. They certainly warrant more than superficial consideration.

At the same time, we need an open mind to explore situations where an applicant acted according to sound principles and what was morally and professionally correct, only to be "punished" by the organisation. Let's make sure we have a broad and sound understanding of the situation and the factions involved.

One of the most destructive influences in a workplace is the corrosive personality. It is not for long discussion here, being a complex issue in itself. But look for the person who is particularly charming and persuasive, presents a most impressive CV, is vague with details (especially about matters which do not support their cause), claims credit for some outstanding (unbelievable?) achievements, is dismissive of the contribution made by others, but able to insinuate that

15

they were the cause of all faults and failures. Remember what is said about something being "too good to be true"!

When we think back to the people we have worked with and the interviews we have conducted, most of us would be happy to work again with people who manifest the three essential qualities of competence, compatibility and integrity to a substantial degree. Those we would definitely avoid would have shown a distinct lack in at least one of them.

3

PREPARATION AND ANALYSIS

Preparation—The Vital Difference

MY dentist says to me, "You don't have to floss all your teeth, only the ones you want to keep." The variation about interviews is this: "You don't have to prepare for every interview, only the ones where you don't want to lose your best applicants."

Applicants have a right to expect us to be fully prepared. They also have a right to be provided with a calm, courteous and structured environment in which to present themselves at their best. What preparation is "necessary and sufficient"? And how should we go about it?

First, we need to develop a basic understanding of each applicant's background by looking at their CV. Then we look more closely, initially for obvious details like qualifications and current role, and then for other matters requiring further discussion.

For example:

- Are there any discrepancies among significant dates?
- Is there evidence that essential selection criteria (such as qualifications and accreditations) have been completed or awarded? Or are they still a "work in progress"?
- Are there any identifiable patterns or trends in the applicant's working or personal life?

At this stage, we should briefly record our positive impressions as well as our concerns. Both will need to be given time and attention in the interview.

Analysis of Patterns and Trends

After the interview, we need to do some sifting and sorting, joining the dots and putting the pieces of the puzzle together. This can be done thoroughly and effectively by displaying all the information we've gathered from the CV and the interview on a Patterns and Trends Table (as described on pages 21-23)

The process is not intended to be a gratuitous delving into the personal life of an applicant. By arranging our information in this format, we are better able to identify areas where further discussion is warranted because of the way incidents or developments in one part of our lives frequently have repercussions or flow-on effects in others. The influence might be beneficial; it might be unfortunate. The fact remains that when competence, compatibility and integrity need to be analysed with a high degree of accuracy and reliability, this approach has been shown to provide more robust insights than others.

For example, frequent changes of "Location" can result from work assignments, the need to look after others, financial difficulties, termination of employment for whatever reason, and many other factors. We need to know. And when patterns start to become apparent, we need to be confident that our understanding is correct. It is not recommended that we make decisions about a person based on a single incident. However, we are likely to be making sound decisions when we have detected, explored and analysed a pattern or trend.

Let us confirm also that the patterns and trends can lead us to see greater strength and resourcefulness than otherwise expected, or they can raise doubts about the individual's suitability. With a Patterns and Trends Table, doubts can be explored both objectively and equitably.

The Patterns and Trends Table is especially helpful when:

- Several applicants appear to be well qualified for the position.
- Panel members are equally divided in their support for two "front-runners".
- The appointment is for a highly sensitive role in which the competence, compatibility and integrity of the appointee will have far reaching effects.

It is amazing how much can be gleaned from both the application and the interview with the use of such a basic structure. (Well, it's not really amazing: it just works, like any sound but simple analytical process.)

As employers, we owe it to ourselves to ensure the interview goes well. Think of the time we have already invested in the whole process. Why would we degrade it now? Would a surgeon insert only half the required sutures because there was a meeting to attend?

Staying calm and structured makes the interview more productive while illustrating the high professional standard of our workplace. And this is precisely the way we would like to be perceived.

Constructing a Patterns and Trends Table

The Patterns and Trends Table will have about seven columns headed with the factors listed below.

The column on the far left is reserved for significant dates in the applicant's life/career, beginning with the most recent. Every date entered into this column represents the start of a new row. Not every cell on every row will be relevant to the issue at hand, though a lack of information in certain cells can serve as a reminder to pursue those matters at a subsequent interview.

If using a computer, try to limit the Table to one screen, so that all the information remains visible at all times. If making a hand-written version, do not hesitate to tape a second page to the bottom of the first. Why is it so important to keep all the information visible? Because it is only by considering **all factors in relation to one another at the same time** that we are likely to generate reliable insights to help us identify the best person for the job.

Make sure you record the applicant's name and contact details before adding any data to your Table.

Factors

- Month/Year: Start with current month and year. Work back. If a specific date seems important, record it (dd/mm/yy) in the relevant cell.

- Profession/Career: Roles and major experiences in profession/career. Make sure month and year are recorded for commencing and terminating each role, including internal postings or appointments, assignments and projects.

- Education/Qualifications: Education, study and other professional development activities, both self-initiated and those made available through employer, etc. Ensure such activities were completed and note what qualifications were actually awarded. Include professional accreditation and memberships.

- Location: Town, area of residence. Housing status— renting, purchasing, etc. Confirm dates and reasons for moving. Follow through when the moves appear random or simplistic.

- Close Personal: Substantial relationships—marriage; separation/divorce; birth of children; serious illness or death of a significant family member; significant issues for a partner; notable family occurrences; etc.

- Financial: Significant financial matters—debts, commitments, inheritances, increases or decreases in remuneration and reasons for same, etc.

- Social: Socio-economic status, contacts, community involvement, etc.

The factors in the Table can be adjusted to suit the circumstances and the role being filled. However, they should not be watered down for significant roles. Many inappropriate appointments at senior level would have been avoided if the interviewers had not been embarrassed to explore them.

4

PRODUCTIVE
INTERVIEWING

THE processes discussed in this section do not involve manipulation or deceit. They are designed to facilitate engagement and the level of communication necessary for an effective interview.

Establish Trust

Here there are lessons for us from those brilliant people who negotiate successfully with hostage takers. From first contact they seek to establish trust, which they do through finding issues of common interest, speaking in an open and non-accusatory manner, and staying calm while listening and responding to the hostage taker. Over time, the degree of engagement tends to increase and a certain amount of trust becomes evident. The same goes for the job interview: these basic principles work equally well in establishing productive rapport in a relatively short space of time.

Remain Impartial

In listening to applicants, we need to be wary of the "halo" effect—in other words, allowing one piece of favourable information to enhance our judgment of an applicant's skills to a level well beyond their actual capabilities. I once saw a bookbinder shortlisted for a job for which he had no qualification, skills or experience. Why? Because bookbinding was a very rare trade and he talked enthusiastically about it!

Conversely, it is not unknown for an applicant's level of capability to be downgraded on the basis of a minor negative observation.

Respond to Signs of Distress

Many people are nervous in interviews, especially at the beginning. It can be evident in awkward actions (e.g. dropping things), sweating (including the handshake), being distracted, asking us to repeat the question frequently, speaking too quickly, making "cannot remember" responses regarding significant issues—for example, an applicant who couldn't remember the major field of study for the Masters degree supposedly awarded within the past five years.

Such cases of "nerves" don't necessarily indicate that the applicant is unsuitable, and it is the interviewer's responsibility to alleviate the stress through calm, open, single questions and encouraging discussion. We might slow down our own rate of speech a little, extend our introduction and encourage the applicant to talk a little more about familiar things in the early stages of our discussion.

Some of the people we would love to have on our team might never have been to a job interview before. Wouldn't it be a shame to lose them because they were not good at something that is rarely seen among the selection criteria.

Ask Open Questions

We all know it, but it never hurts to remind ourselves. Most of the best questions commence with one of the following: *Who, What, Why, When, How,* and *Where*. With a little forethought and practice, we can learn to use those words naturally to phrase our questions.

And there are variations. Instead of saying "Why did you do that?" we can ask "And your reason for doing that was ...?" with the tone of voice adding the question mark. It is still an open question and might fit into the flow of conversation more naturally.

Take care to avoid closed questions (the type that generate only "Yes" or "No" answers) as they have the effect of closing down the dialogue you are trying so hard to maintain. The following are some examples:

Did you do that to get more experience?

Were you happy to leave?

Are you pleased you did that?

Limit Multi-layered Questions

Generally, it is more productive to ask one question at a time and then follow up with exploration of associated issues. However, it can be reasonable to ask a multi-layered question if the role itself typically requires people to acknowledge what is happening, store information, prioritise issues, look for interactions between variables, and take corrective action with vital systems—all in one unflustered sequence of actions. For example, ICU specialists; airline pilots; those who have to deal with the media regularly; leaders of SWAT teams; and others.

Don't Use Hypotheticals

Many of us have enjoyed shows of various types where individuals or teams are challenged with a progressive series of hypothetical problems. Some of us even fancy ourselves as a potential host of such a show. But the job interview is not the place to start!

So no hypothetical questions, none at all! This point cannot be over emphasised! The reason? If you ask a hypothetical question, you will get a hypothetical answer. The response tends to come right out of the textbook and we learn nothing about the applicant's knowledge or experience. And that is a waste of everyone's time.

By the way, hypothetical questions are not legitimised by building a whole scenario around them. That just makes them worse—and you will get an even more convoluted, but still hypothetical, response.

Now, a useful type of question to ask, instead of a hypothetical, will be in a form such as:

In roles such as this one, decisions often have to be made quickly, sometimes even before all the information is available. Could you please describe a recent situation where you had to make such a decision?

Even the applicant's choice of example can be as interesting as the explanation of how she/he managed the whole process.

Further questions can be asked to obtain necessary detail. For example:

How happy were you with the overall outcome?

Considering that as a learning opportunity, what would you do differently in similar circumstances?

This is not a hypothetical question; it allows the applicant to demonstrate a capacity for self-insight and professional reflection in the context of a real situation.

A similar opening question could be:

What types of emergencies have you had to deal with in your job over the past couple of years?

When applicants talk about recent actual experiences, they present a more real account of their own attributes and almost always create the pathway for further constructive discussion. Their response may well add to our understanding of the patterns and trends in the way they operate. If no meaningful example is forthcoming, we need to take that into account also.

Probe Beyond the Headlines

Headlines in the media influence our opinions disproportionately: they can shape reactions much more powerfully than several paragraphs of text.

Some people talk in "headlines". With a positive tone of voice and expressive body language, they focus on just one or two elements that attract attention. As we know, the tone of voice and body language convey more of a message than the words. The bookbinder we mentioned was such an example in a positive sense.

Similarly in an interview, "headlines" can create a much greater impact than the substance of the story. For example:

> *The paper I delivered became the focal point for discussion throughout the whole conference.*

> *Up to that time no one had achieved both goals within the same financial year.*

Both assertions sound impressive but what is the substance behind them?

An applicant for a graduate position was asked the question, "Could you please describe one of the greatest achievements in your life."

The response was a very enthusiastic account of a two week group project to help people in a village in a third world country, waxing eloquent about how they bonded amongst themselves, how they related to the people of the village and what a wonderfully uplifting experience it was.

The interviewer then "probed beyond the headlines" and asked, "And what did you accomplish? What did you contribute to the lives of those people in the village?"

After several attempts to avoid the question and some awkward silences, the actual answer was "nothing"!

It is useful to think of statements or initial responses as a "headline", a gift from the applicant. Why a gift? Well, if it was a response to a good, open question, the applicant is telling us probably much more than she/he thinks while offering us an opportunity to continue the dialogue as well.

Questions which go beyond the headlines include:

What was the actual outcome?

Who was the person accountable on a day-by-day basis?

What were the criteria for success?

How did the actual cost compare to the original budget?

What benefit was gained compared to the cost involved?

Do Not Lead the Witness

When an applicant has made a favourable impression overall, but some of their responses are not as strong as they could be, it is not unusual for an interviewer to put words in an applicant's mouth or "lead the witness", so to speak.

For example, when an applicant has just answered a question about dealing with a complex emergency as a team leader, but has not mentioned how communications were managed, or authority and accountability delegated, we need to ensure she/he has the required experience by seeking further detail, but without prompting them in any way.

At this point it is perfectly acceptable to ask:

Is there anything else you would like to add?

However, we would be **leading the witness** if we asked:

And how did you manage communications?
Or

How were authority and accountability delegated?

Asking such specific questions would suggest to applicants that their thoughts on communication and delegation are important to us and enables them to give a more detailed answer than they would otherwise have been able to provide.

The Value of Silence

Let us never forget the incredible contribution of silence in an interview because it frequently reduces the temptation to "lead the witness". When we let the person finish what she/he is saying and just wait without rushing in with our next question, we often get freely offered and relevant information. This occurs especially when there is more to come but the person is unsure whether to mention it or not. In most people there is a propensity to tell the whole story which is lost when the interviewer immediately asks another question or prompts a particular type of response.

What is said after the silence is not always negative: it can reinforce the applicant's suitability considerably.

For example, suppose we have asked an applicant why she/he left a job after a short period of time and the response was along the lines of *"I loved the job, but there were other factors that also had to be considered ..."* s-i-l-e-n-c-e.

Our own silence, whilst maintaining empathetic eye contact, says we are interested to know more. And the additional information the person was hesitating over could have been any in a broad range. For example:

The immediate supervisor was corrupt or of a corrosive personality.

She/he (our applicant) was not able to meet the job requirements and

... had the good sense to resign, or

... was terminated.

Or it could mean our applicant sacrificed "the perfect job" because she/he considered the needs of another person to be greater; for example, a partner, parent, child, etc. But in the interview she/he was unsure about how that decision would be viewed.

Or there were other conflicts or issues in the applicant's life which she/he does not want to discuss; for example, financial, personal, relationships etc.

There are so many potential scenarios behind unfinished responses; almost invariably it is well worthwhile to give your applicant the time and receptivity to explain.

By the way, applicants who feel the need to withhold the full truth often respond with a comment such as:

It was a personal matter, or

I'm sorry but that was a security issue I cannot discuss, or something similar.

Most interviewers or panels then tend to back off very quickly with apologies for having even asked the question. It is more professional to progress the matter with something like:

We understand that, but for our purpose today we need a clearer understanding of how that matter affected your work and professional commitments. Could you please give us some context and tell us a little more.

(It is always possible for the person to do so and give us the opportunity to verify what they say through other sources.)

Then we try to resume the normal conversational tone of the interview and accept what is said in a non-judgmental way. The information is taken into account in the overall picture, but only rarely should it become the sole or major reason for a decision.

Confirm Details

Whilst we do not wish to put words in an applicant's mouth, we do need to confirm that the information we have recorded is correct. After an applicant has given his or her response, we can summarise the key points she/he has made. This shows the applicant we are genuinely interested and encourages further input from them.

This is an example of how we might go about it.

When something just had to be done, you were not the project leader but made some suggestions which were ignored.

When the leader left, you were given the challenge of fixing the problem and you did it your way.

Your method worked but you were advised to seek prior approval in the future.

Have I got all that right?

Is there anything else you'd like to add?

We note any changes and check that the fresh information is consistent with other data. The process for confirming our understanding does not give applicants any indicator of other issues we would like them to address, but it does give them a fair chance to add points which come to mind as we run through the summary.

Revisit Gaps

At times it would seem that an applicant does not intend to give a full and open account of their career background.

Repeating questions about the same issue or coming back to an issue during an interview helps us gain more information or greater clarity when needed.

If a sensitive issue is introduced within its context, the brain is often alerted to release a customary response. When questions about the same issue are raised out of context or unexpectedly, there is some greater tendency to offer a more complete and accurate response. This works powerfully with returning to a matter subsequent to the first discussion, even in a later interview.

As the interviewer(s) we almost always have the opportunity to gather corroborating evidence, for example, reference checking when done well; inviting an applicant back for a second interview in a more relaxed or congenial environment; or seeking confirmation from a third party—in other words, "doing the research" on the applicant's experience and achievements. When there is appropriate engagement with the referee, we can discover more about the applicant's attitudes and typical behaviour. We just need to keep in mind what the perspective or intent of the referee might be!

Allow Time for Reflection

When an interview is coming to an end, we can invite the applicant to leave the room and wait in a pleasant, quiet place, perhaps with the offer of a tea or coffee. We tell them we will call them in for a couple of final points shortly.

The interviewer(s) then review the information they have collected and identify any matters that need more discussion.

Meanwhile, even without it being suggested, the applicant will reflect on how the interview went, including responses they wished they had expressed better and questions about the job or the organisation they would have liked to pursue.

When the applicant returns both she/he and the interviewer or panel are in a better position to pursue important matters and there can be more candour in the discussion. This is an excellent opportunity to once again raise issues where there appears to be some confusion for whatever reason. Having confidence about the clarity and accuracy of our information is essential for a wise selection decision.

5

PANEL INTERVIEWS

Roles of Panel Members

PANEL interviews can be highly effective if they are planned and managed well. Many are not. There is often an unfounded expectation that every panel member has to ask at least one question or cover one area. There is no sound basis for this. Panel members often make assumptions—for example, that there is no need to pursue a certain matter because the other panel members have not. The Chairperson can "hold court" rather than using low key controls which are more effective.

And you can just have too many on the panel–like the legendary group of fourteen people who all insisted on their right to participate. It wasn't a job interview, it was a cocktail party—without the alcohol for the time being.

Three is an appropriate number of panel members: a Chairperson, a technical/professional expert, and one who monitors the information obtained in relation to the key selection criteria. That member's summary can be crucial in joining the dots to produce a comprehensive and coherent understanding of the applicant's suitability. In fact, the third member does not necessarily have to ask any questions at all!

There is a strong case for having such an "observer", i.e. an experienced person who monitors the coverage of the selection criteria and looks for both themes and gaps in the applicant's responses. With the observer focusing on the content of the repsonses and the reactions of the applicant (including tone of voice and body language) considerable insight can be gathered. More information is frequently gained when one of the panel members does not have to worry about asking questions, and observations can be shared during the period when the applicant leaves the room for a short time.

The "observer" can be the scribe for the interview, but must be much more experienced than the average scribe who might simply record what the applicant says.

Procedures

Most panel members find the procedures simple and relevant; there are not many but adhering to them will give us a better result.

Every panel member must read the application prior to the interview. Before the applicant enters, the chair summarises relevant matters and leads a **short** discussion about what issues appear to need the greatest exploration. It is essential that the Chair **not** show preferences or pass judgments in relation to any of the applicants. It helps if there is some agreement amongst the panel members about whether extra questions are to be asked as they occur or kept until the end.

We have dealt earlier with having a short break in the closing stages of the interview to identify matters about the applicant which are not yet clear enough.

Once the interview has been concluded and the applicant has left, it is time for panel members to make their evaluation.

This must take place **in silence**. There must be no comment from anyone until each has **written** a short evaluation and decision, at least to the point of either "Shortlist" or "Not Suitable". Then the discussion takes place. Keep in mind the different perspectives of the various panel members—some being more technical, some more focused on other attributes.

And in allocating weightings to the various selection criteria it pays to keep in mind a saying from those in the business of recruitment and selection:

"People are hired for their qualifications and experience; they are fired for their attitudes and behavior."

6

COMMON LISTENING TRAPS

DESPITE our best intentions, it is easy for interviewers to fall prey to the following listening traps:

We hear what we want to hear

If our first impression of an applicant is positive, most of us interpret what they say as a confirmation of that original impression. For example, if an applicant is personable and says that she/he "worked with" a highly regarded person, we tend to take that as confirmation of expertise in the applicant. To avoid this tendency we need to gather **all** necessary information before making any decisions.

We make assumptions

And why? Because it is usually easier to accept what we've heard than probe for further details by asking "difficult" or "embarrassing" questions. Yet these questions can be asked without turning the interview into an interrogation. Detailed advice on avoiding this trap can be found in "Probe Beyond the Headlines" pages 29 to 31.

We misinterpret the directive that *"Everyone must be treated the same"*

This directive does not support equitable treatment; it is a cop-out by those who would over-simplify the job interview and make their decisions based on minimal substantial data. The correct thing to do, of course, is to treat each person as an individual. Yes, each one of them deserves to be assessed according to the same criteria and with the same open attitude on our part, but the exploration of their suitability should be based on their individual background. One applicant might have more qualifications, another more extensive experience. It is not appropriate to ignore the strengths of an applicant just because others do not have equivalent achievements or experiences.

We think of the interview as an inquisition

At times an interviewer might ask questions in a way that causes applicants to feel that a deliberate attempt is being made to trap them. There is even the occasional interviewer who believes this is the only way to extract the truth! But there is never a need to be devious or manipulative. A good interviewer can elicit more than enough useful information through open questions, listening, and a disciplined but personable approach. And that sends the right message about your enterprise to the people attending the interview—those you want to have as trusting and trustworthy members of your team.

7

COMMON ASSUMPTIONS

FREQUENTLY, interviewees make assumptions that skew their responses. The following are commonly observed.

Some assume we only want to hear good news

So they tell us what they think we want to hear. For example, when asked about past mistakes, an applicant might avoid admitting they ever made one. But we all know that everyone makes mistakes from time to time. What really matters is the way we deal with our mistakes and what we learn from them. The interviewing techniques described in Section 4 provide guidance on managing this obstacle.

Some believe the job interview is all about first impressions and having a "few laughs"

This situation is more likely to occur when an applicant knows one or more of the interview panel (though I once met a recruiter who believed his assessment of applicants should always include reference to whether or not they had a few laughs). To manage this tendency to trivialise the interview, we need to demonstrate a certain formality in manner and a clearly structured approach. In this way the applicant will be made aware we are doing them the courtesy of taking their interview seriously and that we expect them to do the same.

Some do not expect to be asked to support their claims

If we do not pursue the evidence for the applicant's claims, the interview is unlikely to be effective. For example an applicant might tell us they were awarded "Staff Member of the Month" on several occasions but, when asked, have difficulty explaining the criteria on which the award was based. The solution is to ask questions: for example, whether it went to several people at the same time; or if, over a twelve month period, everyone in that workplace was given a turn. Further advice can be found in Section 4, "Productive interviewing" pages 24 to 38

8

CLOSING REFLECTIONS

Encourage Positive Talk

MANY of us have been brought up with the admonition not to "boast" about ourselves; but that often gets translated in our own minds as an injunction against talking positively about our achievements.

We can help those applicants who find it awkward to talk about their own achievements. Here are a few pointers, not necessarily in order of importance:

What were the high priorities for the organisation last year?

In hindsight, why was a change considered necessary?

What contributed to such a change for the better?

Note that the applicant is not being asked to talk about themselves; the discussion is about events with which she/he would be familiar. Then through encouraging questions, keep the applicant focused on **their** thinking, decisions and achievements. For example:

*How did **you** change the process?*

What did you do differently? (If previous attempts had not been effective.)

What were you accountable for at that time?

What did you learn from the experience?

With these follow-up questions the person usually becomes focused on what was achieved and how, making it is much easier for them to explain their role and contribution.

If the person has received a significant award, published a paper or book, or received some other form of public acknowledgement, we can ask them to talk us through it. Those who are shy about their own achievements often respond with, *"It was nothing really ..."* However, using a calm and encouraging tone of voice, our response can be along the lines of:

> *"Well those awards have a well-deserved reputation and they are not offered without good cause. We know it can be somewhat embarrassing, but please tell us a little more."*

Then without gushing (and causing more embarrassment) we can show genuine interest, leave time for the applicant to tell the story without asking questions too quickly and move the focus onto the professional issues rather than the personal.

In summary we can help people by talking about what they **did**, rather than what **they** did. Talking about outcomes, technical challenges, and problem solving is often more comfortable for the applicant, and we get the important information we need.

Beware Those Who Ignore the Rules

If an applicant ignores the rules _now_, seems not to understand what issues you want them to address, or reveals a pattern of counter-productive choices in previous employment, what are the chances they will work cooperatively in your team once appointed?

We have all seen interviewers agonising over "giving the benefit of the doubt" to such applicants and hypothesising reasons for their attitudes. The more realistic response is found in the maxim: "When in doubt, don't!"

9

THE LAST WORD

TRUE!

And the final word is "Encourage".

Let us encourage ourselves and other interviewers to keep getting better; encourage our applicants to engage with us and with the process; encourage the panel and the authorities to allocate the time and resources a good appointment deserves.

We are dealing with a myriad of personalities. So, reflection teaches us much for future efforts. There is always something we have not come across before, something more to learn.

Let us enjoy the job interview. When we do, we provide leadership for the panel; the applicant gets exclusive time and attention (and isn't that a treat); and the interviewers get to develop and use some special interpersonal skills.

It is well worth becoming expert interviewers—who will never be heard muttering to ourselves, *"But in the interview ...!"*

Printed in Australia
AUHW011359151019
318625AU00001B/4

9 780994 615596